In the Cosmic Fugue

In the Cosmic Fugue

Poems by

Jocelyn Heath

© 2022 Jocelyn Heath. All rights reserved.
This material may not be reproduced in any form, published,
reprinted, recorded, performed, broadcast,
rewritten or redistributed without
the explicit permission of Jocelyn Heath.
All such actions are strictly prohibited by law.

Cover design by Shay Culligan
Cover image by Fred Moon via Unsplash

ISBN: 978-1-63980-202-9

Kelsay Books
502 South 1040 East, A-119
American Fork, Utah 84003
Kelsaybooks.com

For my family, chosen and blood

Acknowledgments

My thanks to the journals below for publishing some of the poems in this volume, with occasional variations in content or title:

Aeolian Harp, Vol. 4: "Self-Portrait as a Black Hole," "Orbital," "Tower"
Bellingham Review: "In the War Museum"
Crab Orchard Review: "Plaza in Late Spring," "Orbital" (winner of the 2014 Allison Joseph Poetry Award)
Fourth River: "Letter from Anacostia Park"
The National Poetry Review: "Self-Portrait as a Black Hole"
Natural Bridge: "Nomenclature," "Love Poem for San Antonio"
New Mexico Review: "Night Drive to the Mountains"
Poet Lore: "Shell-Gathering in the Keys"
Poetry South: "Epithalamion"
Sinister Wisdom: "The Galaxy Is a Lesbian Dance Night," "The Girl with Violets on Her Lap," "Tower"

I have many to thank for helping this book come into being, beginning with those whose teaching helped me grow: Cleis Abeni, Elizabeth Spires, Elizabeth Arnold, David Bottoms, Michael Collier, Julie Enszer, Stanley Plumly, Tan Lin, Matthew Olzmann, Alicia Stallings, Leon Stokesbury, and Natasha Trethewey. My classmates at University of Maryland, especially Jennifer Voyles and Katherine Young. My classmates at Georgia State University, especially Marcela Fuentes, Stephanie Devine, Rachel Wright, Kelly Neal, Mike Saye, Brian Heston, Andrea Rogers, and Valerie Gilreath. My colleagues at Norfolk State University. Katy Gurin, for reading.

Special thanks to my professor and mentor Dr. Beth Gylys, for her guidance and unwavering faith in my work; to my parents (Roy and Barbara Heath), who encouraged my creativity from day one; and most of all to my wife, Michelle, and our son Hunter—thank you for being my reasons to write.

The author also wishes to acknowledge the inspiration for the book's title and title poem, *Cosmos* by Carl Sagan.

Contents

I

Out of Chaos	15
Self-Portrait as a Gas Giant	16
Inner Ring	17
Outer Edges	18
Tower	21
Binary Stars	22
That Other Girl	23
Suburban Ghost Stories	24
Veiled Planet	28
In the War Museum	29
Clippings	31
Neptune's Pursuit	32
Cul-de-Sac Rules	33
Dark Nebula	35

II

Syzygy	39
Evolution	40
Jupiter, Unyielding	41
Letter Home	42
Terra Nova	44
First Contact	45
Orbital	46
The Girl with Violets in Her Lap	47
In the Cosmic Fugue	48
Self-Portrait as a Black Hole	49

III

Self-Portrait as Supernova	53
The Galaxy Is a Lesbian Dance Night	54
Love Poem in a T.G.I. Friday'	55

First Time	56
Night Drive	57
Late Storm	58
Study in Orchids	59
Love Poem for San Antonio	60
Hydromancy	61
Wormhole Retrospective	62
Gaia	63
Shell-Gathering in the Keys	64

IV

Letter to Kepler 452b	67
Study in Rare Blooms	68
Studies in Lepidopterae	69
Nomenclature	71
H Street Aubade	72
What We Have Left	74
Deep Space	75
Study in Aquatics	76
Letter from Her, Anacostia Park	77
Letter to Her, Written on a Washing Machine	78
Letter to Her, with Map Turtle	79
Letter from the Airport at Midnight	80
Epithalamion	81
Unearthed	83
Plaza in Late Spring	84

I

Out of Chaos

Meteors are sugar
        amid planetary gravel
this asphalt galaxy under
        bare feet. I walk over
multitudes curb to curb
        infinite
what I can be, they say;
        infinite the colors
on homes cut from one die
        a spiral orbit on a cul-de-sac.
Infinite parents driving home
        calling us in
lights in evening windows
        ebb and flow toward this
inlet of a cosmic ocean
        in which we dip bare toes
oblivious to the possible
        beyond this our known universe.

Self-Portrait as a Gas Giant

Astronomy for kids:
big is bad. The
class giggles at Uranus,
draws farts at the
edge of the worksheet.
Fat marker in my hand, a
growing belly-
hurt, I color Saturn
inside the lines. *If you
just try*—; all the advice I
keep trying cycles in my mind.
Lunch is an asteroid belt I
maneuver badly, get a seat but
no peace as my belly expands to
otherworldly dimensions while the
pretty girls keep small.
Recess I spend alone under a tree,
skimming my book,
tracing Jupiter's red eye
until the whistle blows.
Vast planets attract moons
while my orbit stays empty.
Exile squeezes like pants
you just can't
zip anymore.

Inner Ring

They lick up her debris,
gulp the sweet, sour, bitter

as she throws it down.
Throats shredded

heal quick but cratered, chatter on.

Unmissable, their table
beside a bright yellow stage.

I would lay my diamond heart
ring at her feet. I send slices

of apple cake spangled
with sugar. The plate returns

not even crumbs.

Outer Edges

I.

Girl on the moor.
Girl in flight, feet crushing
dead heather into scrub,
through endless fog.

Boy on the moor.
Boy in pursuit, mud-slicked,
sprinting, hands dropping like swallows
onto her shoulders.

They tumble through dead grass.
He leans heavy on her arms,
wriggles up to take his kiss.

II.

In a birch copse playhouse
at the field's edge,
a play family wakes:

children curled on leaves,
the Mother and the Father
behind the farthest trunk

wave them away to school, slip
behind the white trunk wall,
retreat into the leaf-dark chamber.

Girl, the curious always-child,
doubles back to listen.

III.

Where boxwood shrubs
draw up tight
and close out the rain,
a refuge worth
the crawl through
dense branches
to the clearing within.
They lie down upon
the dry grass.

Only the Girl sees what they do.
The leaves swallow sighs
and so does she.

IV.

Girl in the field.
Girl at the borders
of the game:

boys chasing girls,
catching braids, shirts,
whole bodies

in their swinging arms,
lips pressed quick
to whatever they can reach.

Boys claim the copse,
drive the girls giggling into
the thicket.

She is rarely chased.
She knows what that means.

Tower

One red bloom
with petals of a child's fingertip's breadth
suspended by a broken trellis over

a concrete square stained with rust,
beside the brief slope flecked
with dust and mica bordering

a kingdom around a vine-wrapped tower.
The blue ribbed doll blanket laid out on a corner
makes a bed. In the beach bucket,

we stir a goulash of leaves and dirt.
My friend imagines that she is a prince
and we lie down,

the double yellow center of the rose
above us an eye leaning ever closer.

Binary Stars

Heartbeat orbitals
two-stepping through galaxies

blue heat rhythm strip
a reliable calculus

beyond any gaze
but undeviant—

inseparable, the pairing
we learn to want young

to be one of the two;
take comfort in coupling

declared universal if only
for these stars, this dance

That Other Girl

has a body no deeper than a cracker box

has just a toss of freckles on her nose

wears curls or crimps or two French braids

has hips the width of a story book

wears leggings and pleated skirts

rubs on fruit punch lip balm after lunch

has glittery shoelaces and pierced ears

is what our teacher calls *lithe*

dangles from the monkey bars

sits in a classroom down the hall

sits in my orbit if I take a wide loop

doesn't know I am her satellite

Suburban Ghost Stories

1.

On the rainbow bars at recess,
Kathryn says, *at night, I visit Heaven.*
Her spirit goes as the body sleeps.

No chain links of sin disinvite her—
her spirit dines in tidy white.
She says, *I think you may be worthy.*

She says few may come and go
and have the proof while on Earth by day.
An invite: from God through her,

they'll drop the links I never knew I had
so I may visit. (What could I have done?)
That night, I dream nothing,

then am told my spirit laughed
too loud, stained her gown, left in shame.
(No. I speak softly. How could it be true?)

2.

Here, homes are stamps
pressed to the earth
from mixed ink pads.

No crumble of castle wall
or quarry's edge; nothing old
but the land itself.

We roam, scab our knees
on maple bark, speed our bikes
down every driveway.

A white pine grove
shaded even at noon:
we swear the air's colder.

We *know* we feel things
brush our arms. We flee
our dreamed-up ghosts.

3.

There's never a name but all know
the one who went into the woods
never returned. Or did,
bloodied and rent. Or
reappeared as bone
and rag in a creek bed.
(Aren't trails meant for walks?)
Go as one, you're done.
Go as two, you might live through.
Shadows stretch toward sidewalks
as if to say, *trust us.*
The paved path wanders in
and vanishes.

4.

Beech leaves snowed softly on the hillside
behind our homes: wide field of golden weeds
bright in the fading sun. Tall grass flattened
into channels and chambers that we entered
before we knew we had. A turn in the meadow:
remains of fire and three cracked dishes:
niche in the tall grass: old mattress.
Rusting shadows smear its print roses.
That night, we were told of glass and needles
and men who lurched toward those who entered.
After, we could only watch the weeds in the breeze.

5.

Years later, I read in the paper
a guy from my 8th grade bus
got shot and tracked his blood
from footpath to parking lot
then died. I'd dared to bike
into those woods that spring.
Heart pounding at hill's crest,
I lifted feet from pedals to fly—
this landing, startling and hard.

6.

In fourth grade, I read ghost stories.
On the phone, Kathryn tells me
a house in the woods near hers
is haunted. *We can go see it.*

I think—it's gray stone from long ago.
Or is it wood, browned to leaf-shade
like old barns on the highways?
I think of ponds and weeping willows
and the pull of ghostly Helen

in the book I read last weekend,
snarling a child in weeds so the water
took her breath. I ask my father
so I can be forbidden.

Veiled Planet

It hides in milky sulfur clouds
        its red rock heart.
Telescopes see Venus as Earth's twin
        shrouded with a heated veil—
rarely, the pocks and pitting. You could miss
        the smoldering cones that burst lava
like blackheads and mar the surface.
        We only think we know it.

In the War Museum

London, 1993

When we come out of the netted shelter,
smells of bitter smoking meat

from the replica road, where a vinyl girl
lies tucked under rumpled concrete:

no time to close her eyes.
If she could see, the dome of St. Paul's

still stands on the opposite wall,
rosy with destruction.

These bricks chip a little more
each time the benches rattle.

To our south, Yugoslavia cracks
like the shell of an overboiled egg.

In today's paper, a blue bundle shoved to a curb.
The sheet sprouts two hands, soiled

to black, clenched
against a concave belly.

I see the word my father hollows out
when he reads to us

from our Bible stories book:
it's when a man hurts a woman

in a way he never should.
The false smoke rises from this street.

After, in the quiet silver stall, a streak
of smoky blood rushes out of me.

Clippings

Up, up above, the ecstatic swirl of wasps.
Belly, thighs, hips, the spaces between.
I measure myself with fingers:
a hurt necessary as the gravel in my back.
Unfold the topography of a woman:

cleft of freckled breast,
cinch of silk at the waist—
photos glisten from sun silvering the hedge
where I hide. Through the summer,
the globed nest swells.

Neptune's Pursuit

God of trident and thrusting current,
god whose wet muscles pin me to sand
and hold me down while you fill
every space of my body—

even your gentlest current drags us out,
leaves known shores unreachable.
Nude god behind a blue planet's drape,
I would fight your saline kiss

and all that followed.
When you clutch a girl in your crests,
with few strokes can she pull her own way.
I do not float willingly.

I toe your edge, touch driftwood fingers,
let a boy swing me in his arms but not keep me.
His white is your foam.
His skin oozes clear salt.

When he moves to swell over me,
I have already swum away.

Cul-de-Sac Rules

1.

Being a girl means dolls in the home
made under the picnic table
that is also often a boat.

It means pom-pom skates
and neon socks stacked
like ice cream scooped on plates.

It means we understand only each other,
means finding the one you want to be like.
Look like. Look at one another—

in the gut, the affirming flutter
means *yes, still her.*

2.

White vans and lollipops:
do not approach.
Parents, schools coach
us on stranger-danger,
walk fast, if change
unsettles you, scream NO.
I rammed a jagged toe
into a boy's shin when
he cornered me, then
ran away. Ask questions later
if you even bother.
What I don't understand
is what to do when the van
is my thought and NO
isn't enough to make it go.

3.

Only when the parents are in bed
do we dare to turn the dead-
bolt, soften the click—
the door sticks—
but we flee through tidy pines,
cars centered in driveway lines.
Our world without its color:
we are smaller.
Stay out of it, we're told, *stay
in.* We have to touch the gray
for ourselves. We can't believe
in danger from shadows. We weave
across lawns and watch for lights—
breathless, her hand in mine.

4.

Don't question what the flutter's about.
Nothing's odd—don't doubt
and say it to a friend, on the phone,
in whispers, to feel less alone.
Say, when she hugs you the next day,
no—it meant nothing. I'm not gay.
Say nothing, ever. It will go away.

Dark Nebula

Black horse in fuchsia sky:
oblique throat birthing stars
that wobble off to orbit.

Brown horse in a ring
orange-lit and lettered
bearing a girl
in fuchsia leggings.

The dark nebula accretes;
spooked, horse charges
toward a fence
but a leap into star-pocked sky.
Grip the opaque neck:

eyes open, racing through
pastures to unknown orbit.

II

Syzygy

Uluru, Australia

We woke at three to catch the sunrise.
What mysteries sleep beneath this sand
as day phosphoresces at the horizon's edge?
A late crescent and star align over the rock,

point to secrets of the desert sand.
What do I think I'll find here?
When star and crescent align
over Uluru, when I can't look away,

do I think that here I'll find
some truth? Far from home, in the night sky
over Uluru? I can't look away:
three bodies fixed in orbit's stasis.

Far from home, in the night sky, truth
in constellations comes human-made
from bodies fixed in orbit. Is stasis
what we're looking for—

our lives made clear like constellations?
I woke at three. I wait for sunrise
wondering what I'm looking for, or if I'll find it
phosphorescing at the horizon's edge.

Evolution

Life scalds
onto planetary faces.
From fissures, legs and arms
kick loose the detritus

of birth. Coupling,
in shrub and shadow
they formed:
man. Woman.

When the sunrise found
two of the same,
breast pairs nested like eggs—
and more—

order ruptured.
Chased into recesses, burned,
they fled. Chose to roll love deep
into the mud of self instead.

Even in caverns,
mica-flecked cheeks
shone. Nascent stars.
Lore, passed in whispers:

unspool their orbits.
Chart those who walk
the periphery of the universe—
find who I am to seek them out.

Jupiter, Unyielding

Lunar muscles round out his arm,
his chest: god of the planet, whose
purple robe trails in stardust
on this glossed page—
my finger edging a thigh
that glides upward to what

I am told I should want.
Turn the page:
moons in a ragged waltz.
In close orbit, Ganymede,
his plump ice-cheeks
blushed with storm-red

rage at being taken—
as the boy of myth caught in air
and caged in lustful talons
to serve his red-eyed master.
Pushed to his knees.
Voice stopped up

by the god's thickness, knowledge
pouring down his throat.
The tenderness after—
I don't understand how
he can embrace the desire
that took him by force.

Letter Home

See this? Like a cut raspberry smudged on my skin,
the long slow pull of a "slipped leg" against the sharp edge.
A tree branch on the way up, outside my dorm window:
hickory, flaking bark into cupped hands.
The long slow peel of a scab to the acrid green beneath.

I sat in that window. I sat in that tree.

All that term I sat and watched
the computer screen swirl top right to bottom left,
top left to bottom right, coming back always
to begin it again. And that's what I couldn't do—
get back to the rhythmic roll of days from hall to hall,
book to book, feigning a search for "the one."
Safe because no disappointment would ever come.

It came to me on the branch of that tree:

first verse of a song I had no theory to write,
no chords to rise and resolve from the lyrics
I fought against singing.

Queer hushed the trees.
Queer hummed the wind.

And when that strange love spreads like fire
through the thicket of veins, boiling eye waters,
choking thought, singeing neurons black, then—
yes, then, you can understand the only way
to put it out was to cut it, vent it through open skin.

Is this what I tell you, now that the match is struck again?
Is this the truth that can jump a fire-cut?
Sit there and read, mother, read one last night in unknowing,
before the touch of my skin will scald you with understanding.

Terra Nova

I hum Earth songs. Pull blankets up
and breathe only my own air in
this desert rushed by worry's heft.

Hissing, whistling bugs
thump my nylon biome, scratch
at threads to chew my skin.

I would take the sting
of mandibles over
the handless company of air

recycled, water passed
through my body over and over,
barely changing.

I would risk
this unmapped plain—
but my courage abandons me too.

Where starship captains broker peace
with fangs, I watch,
from afar, to learn a species.

First Contact

Set a hand to the ground: draw maps in alien dust.

Leaves finger passing shoulders, curl around elbows

as she crushes fringed violets on approach.

Her body made incandescent, your hands are satellites

in its orbit, making her dark places glow with your sweat and dust.

Let her breaths ascend from ankle to thigh

as the evening exhales purple stars

into her thumbed-open nebula.

There will be time later to chart this place—

still, silvery, with light of two waxing moons.

Orbital

The world encased in celestial glass: God's mobile
on a high shelf, whirling. Taken down, set in the sky

and buoyed across space-time. Man inside, hand pressed
to glass, and in the hand, a microscopic calculus of shells

spins a matched rhythm, seeding flesh hedgerows,
growing the very gardens of us.

Or tiny solar systems refracted infinitely across the body,
their galactic turbulence compressed

the way Krishna parted sandy lips to show the universe perched
on his tongue, half-moon and planets circuiting his palate.

Somewhere, satellites spin into the black, snapping neon
afterbirth of stars growing fast, as gas giants

veer close—then depart on their known orbits,
leaving only moons to keep each other company.

On a street, people push-pull to destinations,
flick open half-spheres of umbrellas

or fall into the metal flow of transit,
joining and separating like shared electrons.

As on a laptop screen, moons swing around planets made of variables,
equations swinging fast or slow, large and small bodies

in wide or narrow circles, some close enough to crash—
others far off and cold, never to touch—

a thousand tiny gears wound to run the universe.

The Girl with Violets in Her Lap

I knew the basket of her fingers,
the violet glow

against the underside
of her breasts,

petals thick in the vale
between her thighs.

Spring violets,
white and lilac and purple.

I knew her, Sappho,
before I found your fragments—

the unspeakable excerpted
—and her,

beautiful bride
in her chamber prior to dressing.

Readying herself for one
whose fragment wore away

and set her center on the page
for me to find.

Woman bright with petals,
who I have known but never seen

until flowers fluttered off the page,
and then you—

In the Cosmic Fugue

Static across the starry street;
stars I can find: Orion's belt,
one, two, three.
Infinity above streetlights
a billion voices crackling
like a school hallway
and I only hear:
trust   you can't   someday

And the buzz ramps up
and my mind is a wide white dish
trained at a desert sky
scanning, desperate for sense
but garbling all
(or afraid of garbling)
in a wild search for constellations,
I find no fixed stars.

Self-Portrait as a Black Hole

Astronomers try to explain me,
but I'm relative like E=m
c^2, seen only by what accretes near me:
dwarfs, neon gasses, stellar dust like
Einstein's hair veiling his great brain.
Far off, compressed into my own
gravity, I rotate alone, crushing my
heart to densities
immeasurable by any calculus.
Just walk away when it's too much
knotting of space-time to my will,
lest you implode from the pressure—
molten inside—like me.
No one knows what I've taken in:
oxygen the least of it. So many
protons, particulates,
quarks, quirks, and more in a
radius the sharpest radio telescope hardly
sees. I won't let it see me—
too many try to get close
until they hit dark matter, then
vacillate between us and pleasing the
world. I won't be magnified,
x-rayed, mapped, known by
you or anyone.
Zero divides by nothing.

III

Self-Portrait as Supernova

Zwicky called me *super*—and
you see brightness—but I am
exploding as we speak.
What you see is
vibrancy, my light
unabated until I'm gone.
Telescopes focus on other
stars, but for a moment, I seem to
radiate beyond them all.
Quietly, secretly, I
pass into dust and debris
over eons. There's
no hiding it for long.

Maybe rubble isn't so bad, as
long as all my pieces
keep shining—it's
just that oblivion
is terrifying, so I
hope they write me onto
galactic charts (though I'll burn out
faster than the ink can dry) and
exist forever, somehow.
Don't think I don't know my
chances: I want to be the next
Big Bang, but I'm always
another fallen star.

The Galaxy Is a Lesbian Dance Night

After Tracy K. Smith

The rooms are collapsing:
dark gravity crushes bodies
as exothermic bass humidifies air.
Every corner crammed—
sparkled halters, trucker hats,
and PBR cans constellate the floor.
No place like ours.
One floor of someone else's club—
so many flare up and burn out
before hitting our radar.

Dead center: women collide and orbit.

Fuchsia light, orange, gold, blue—
each beat a shot from Hubble
and just as distant to me.
I'm the shape of a monster
in a starscape of women
too dazzling to approach as I am.
But I can't evade the singularity's pull—
giving into frequencies and thrums
my feet and hips lead me toward
an event horizon I can't cross.

Love Poem in a T.G.I. Friday's

We're back under the pierced glass lamps
where I leaned on her arm and looked
at her driver's license not for the picture
she showed off to our youth group kids
but to check the year of her birth.
(Only four years older.) And it scared
and excited me because suddenly,
she was real, not some imagined love,
and this could, in fact, be. Even now,
my feet drum the booth ready to run
from what's too much, from gentle arms
that clutch tight enough to smother
everything I am. On her couch, we talked
until her hand dared to fix my earring,
smooth my hair and the kiss followed—
I don't know how to do this.
Safe in the din of clinking pints, I watch
her watch the game at the bar TV,
absorbed as I think I could be—
as I think I might let myself be—
in us. The pitcher winds up, releases
the ball he held close, trusting
in the path that he set it on.
I never did learn how to throw.

First Time

Blue candle wax waterfalls
from a sconce,

blue of scented bells
waving in churchyards
an ocean ago.

I am the marker
of a life yet to live.

You wind like ivy
into every crevice
kept miniscule for years,

and split me open.
Wax pools on the floor.

Headboards are tomorrow's
headstones. Now dead,
I sleep until morning.

Night Drive

West Virginia

A chain gang of boxcars drags coal
toward the pipe-latticed power plant
where a long lake glows,
orange on the water like long-ago flames
gouging a row house out of its block
while I watched from my father's arms—
as in this water, those flames multiplied
and lit in the lake a second sky where
for a moment, the sunset—hours past—
returned, broadened, until I saw blaze eclipse lake
and fire charge through water and reeds and grass
to level the woods to my house—
poplars cracking and deer thundering
toward us on the shore lines, vine-snarls falling
as fire cages to trap fawns, block us
on a crescent of sand—and in the doubled sky,
wide wings thrashed their body in spirals,
the soundless screams of smoking feathers
before silhouette dissolved into orange night.
Eyes open to the gray smoke that I couldn't believe
loomed only over that house, fighting my father
as he turned to walk the path back home,
knowing what could follow us there. I never shared
all of this story: just that the chimney
crumbled to ash—the home, a gap and loss.
The power plant glows on as we pass
back into the lightless new-moon night.
I watch ditches and embankments,
the black tree line just beyond the halo
of high beams, for those flicks of motion
that are all the warning we'll get.

Late Storm

Snowmelt off my tongue,
what if, what if—

if wet walls of pine straw turned
a slipped foot into a fatal descent?

Log-split skulls tint rivulets pink.

But do we miss white quartz seams
slicing horizons into mountain laurel,

of waterfalls hidden
in rhododendron valleys,

of sentinel hawks on pines
branching from the cliff's heart?

Out this window, only gray and grass.

Now the speckled sky
makes my point for caution.

We glissade across chill sheets until
she presses down my legs,

stills my burning heels. Pleasure,
or the white rush of falling?

Study in Orchids

Purple blooms glow in shady nooks,
stems coil around branches
but hold themselves ever apart:
watching, weighing.
Water, air, twig, rot: tubers
slip out, searching as the flowers
seem to stay still. Hedging on better,
but holding onto what they have,
surveilling each rock and runnel of soil.
Nothing in this corner,
the roots wind toward another,
creep toward the sliding exit door.

Love Poem for San Antonio

Your umbrellas surprised me every time:
yellow, red, blue, orange framed
in the footbridge's arc.
Green courtyard of the Alamo
edged with bluebonnets and *esperanza*.
Bright city where, left alone, I walked
stirring an iridescent purple drink
with the night souring on my tongue,
closing like a mouth around me—
I watched for hours your little fountains
pouring into the infinite loop of river.
Copper bells along the banks hang still
as those at your old missions,
where this morning I passed through
walls once filled with converts—
the devotees long departed—
and halted by a double archway
full of sky, draped with trailing pink roses,
and lifted a camera not good enough
to capture glints of ore within the rocks
or what it was I wanted to see through.

Hydromancy

What lovers throw into water, after:
house keys, wedding bands that skim,
watches dead or dying—my daffodils
waltz through foam till drowning.

How long until they reach bottom?
Where will the current travel?
I follow to the top of the falls
to hear a hissed answer.

But water drives hard into the pool
bearing the stain of river—
a copper circlet worn too long—
and she's not here to see

how green the water is. This trail runs
along the sides of mountains—
the river follows, turns a slight bend,
and is gone.

Wormhole Retrospective

Age 13: space-time warped.
We crossed the ocean, headed home,
but I crashed on some distant planet.
I studied astrophysics, all alone,

cut from tube and fiberglass a leap
forward—or back, or both?—in time,
forced a tunnel between two points
(or among my alien peers), to align

them, theories, prospects, chance.
I spent nights reading up on space
to learn its secrets. How to travel
back and fix what I fucked up. A place

and time to choose over again. Restart,
repeat. But fractures where I cut
blew shards off, irretrievable, merged
with earthly dust. Lost galaxies. What

vanished with you, I'll always wonder.
I know now the negative pressure, energy—
implosion's risk. A butterfly's wings—
but I built and held a possibility,

kept it for years, dusting the gridded edge,
adding journeys mapped of regret
chasing the infinitesimal radius:
an event horizon that I never met.

Gaia

I bend and reach into my own Earth,
smelling of rainsquall and rose,
to pull my hand up shining.

Your hair, the soil that roots you.
You hold your molten self inside
so you may hold others close:

stone, water, grass, human,
though we look ever elsewhere
and find no brighter star.

From furrowed breast, fruits rise
and thrive. What else have I missed,
looking only to the skies?

Shell-Gathering in the Keys

Unable to leave one shell unchecked
for flush of cream and flame,
unwilling to break the crouch,
knees cut by mussel shards—

I turn over shell after shell,
drive a thumbnail into the grit
to unearth what's half-buried,
divide shard from scallop.

Down the shore,
a man sweeps his metal detector,
checks every buzz from his wand—
can't help a fifth pass at a spot

knowing how the hand trembles
at the thought of gold
and the overlooked treasure
lodges itself deep.

IV

Letter to Kepler 452b

I knew you were out there
even when the math said
divide by 10^{99}
and halve it again
then again;
there's your odds.

Even when they said
there's no perfect match,
that you were a trick
of physics and telescopes,
I sought your sun
in distant skies—
knew there was more
than one of us out there.

There will be time
to map your terrain,
your depths,
brush back the clouds
to learn what inhabits you.

But your brightness
across galaxies
a promise written
in variables—
that's all I need to know
you're out there,
and perfect.

Study in Rare Blooms

Avon Park Air Force Bomb Range

Ashy wilderness
of loose-packed silicate
shell holes sprouting
sweet-scented pigeonwing,
pale mauve.

She reads on leaves
the secret codes
of beetles. In the night,
they scrawl
across the green ribs:

*look, look! Blossom's lips,
modest hood—
dew-tongued flesh, opened, sweet.*
She notes: *clitoria fragrans,
open.*

This flower: intimate pink
of another woman.
Jet engines rattle
a plant, the fence.
That's not what shakes her.

Studies in Lepidopterae

I.

I see her swing the silk net
like a tablecloth, gather it
close. Swing wide,

and let the man-high grass
bend over her—
wave her sail

so it will swoop her up
into the Iowa sun.
Fill it full, pinch it tight,

run the glass over every inch.
A fingertip's brush holds
two dozen flitting wings.

II.

But no. It's night, and mosquitoes tune
in the bandshell of an ear,

echo neon buzz of the light
she hung over a bucket trap.

In the morning, she'll gather moths
dead or dazed from the ethanol,

number and pin them, static
wildflowers blooming on wood.

Tonight, she rises at the sirens,
show the officers her bucketfuls

of wingtips—not meth crystals—
and when they leave,

sinks back into the native grasses,
keeping the vigil, taking her count.

III.

It's like this: she flips leaves on hikes
to see who grows

fat off the chlorophyll,
while I watch glittery cocoons

for the dark wriggle of wings.
I want the burnished aqua

of a tiger beetle and to ask
why its name stripes.

I want dark flutters over
purple petals amid ferns.

She wants to know the culprit
for chewed holes

and dying limbs—to trace it
far into the hornbeams. Together,

we solve the riddle of the bird
gliding white behind the bracken.

Nomenclature

For Michelle

Empty, the sky above, where in daylight a hawk
rode the breeze, so high you could barely name it.

Red-shouldered, you said.
It mattered to you, to call it what it was—
your nomenclature simplified for me—

like the Christmas fern: *Polystichum acrostichoides.*
And the English ivy (*Hedera helix*) that grows
to cover any unfilled space.

And now, we hike the double forest—
trunks dark and shadow-dark—to the pond
where we didn't dare swim in daylight:

stripped and shivering, entering by inches.
Black and silver night, where moonlight
skims across the pond to touch your pale hips—

where our breasts, half-moons at the waterline,
float among waterlogged stars.

H Street Aubade

From your bed, I watch
the same orange light
from the same tall pole,
unblinking as it was
when dusk fell last night
and the night before.
My laptop now shut,
its screen glow imprinted
on the dark with the words:
I am pleased to offer admission
four states south of you.
Last year, I would've left
when the letter came,
but it never did. Instead, you.
This year, a letter holds
all the right words—for then.

On our trip last month,
I watched you watch a waterfall—
rivulets crisscrossed limestone,
water clear and inviting
but frigid with snowmelt.
At that point, we still waited
to hear if I'd have to choose at all.
Your back faced my camera
and I couldn't see what the water
meant to you. Just the cycle of it,
maybe—what falls to the ground
will always rise again and carry on.
I took your picture anyway.

The city clears its rumbling throat
as you stir, but do not wake.
A car rolls down the back alley
and then passes out of thought.

I stay to put off this little leaving
that today hurts as much
as the big leaving I will surely choose.
It's only logical, you said. But nothing
feels quite right. The streetlamp,
in the rising sun, blinks out.

What We Have Left

The hillock of pasta and half-moons of squash,
the cat's short respite on a thigh
and the wood scent of cut dill on hands,
a cardinal high in the tulip tree
and the gray stone knee-deep in the brown creek,
crest of scapula beneath a palm
and the ocean's slow nibble at the tideline
leaving just a sand-sliver and a whelk—
the clink of our rings
into shot glasses on the sill as we wash dishes.
These few months before I go again.

Deep Space

Distance is black and white:
telescopes show each galaxy as a star
on the swath of night.

Unmagnified, we lose sight
of parts in orbit. Heat dissipates
until light-years ice over.

Far from you, I look north.
Then skyward: a thousand thumbtacks
pricking the dark—

a route map to you—
veiled behind orange auras
of urban nights.

Alone in this humid city,
I may as well be
across the Milky Way.

Study in Aquatics

Under lights like moon jellies,
she spreads herself like coral—
her anemone kiss
whorled into my skin.
Having chosen language
over lover, I kick off hard
toward an hours-off home.

By day, she tends her tanks.
Studying each fin and scale,
the increments of change
that could turn foul a wetland
where heron nests thatch
corners of marsh and
mud lips pinch estuaries shut.

Schools of travelers plunge beside me
along stormy kelped highways.
I float in seasons. Unrooted
sea grass roots again if water wills,
the where and how beyond foresight.
But after years adrift, apart,
how can sand and stem reunite?

Letter from Her, Anacostia Park

At lunchtime, I watched the milk jugs
bask with turtles in the mud. The cattails you love
spit fuzzy phlegm into the river, each piece
thickening with diesel and sinking fast.
I walked to the trestle, tossed flags into nests
as reminders to oil the eggs next week.
On the calendar: population control.
Not stealing eggs—they'll just lay more—
but a gentle touch of oil to seal the shell
and fossilize the gosling in its yolk.
I think of honking rage and feathers
—how the mother hisses and dodges blows
from our oars—her ire at the boat misplaced.
When we put the eggs back, glistening, in the nest,
she'll still incubate, unaware of the addled shell-pores
stifling her unborns' breaths. Or perhaps she waits
for the possibility of the tiniest spot missed.
I want, just once, to watch this vigil—her warming
and prodding, the moon and sun cycling across
the black eye. How many times until she knows?
I want to see her take the final flight,
feathers dripping into the water as she goes.

Letter to Her, Written on a Washing Machine

Pretty quarters on the lid: forests, wilder
than the thin seam by your house,
that we long to wander.
Remember Shenandoah?

Wandering the dirt track over a mountain,
trekking to swimming holes
in the gully below: time of mountain laurel,
blue haze afternoon pressing hard

and dripping down our backs.
Clouds raced us to the valley floor.
Let's go. I couldn't help turning one last bend
to find the numbing clear pool—

you read danger in the sky,
but I floated in the sway of fish
past your warnings until
the thunder growled.

My bottle ran dry. My ankle wrenched,
but we ran the graveled ridge
through every gust threatening rain.
I feared the cleave of mountain,

a slicing flash to cut us apart—
your eyes hot
with logic brushed aside
for another five minutes' swim.

Rain that never came.
My last quarter flashes, vanishing.

Letter to Her, with Map Turtle

I confessed, on my visit, to missing
one of her kind in the road—to the pop
of shell and meat beneath a tire.
It happens, you said, because it's true:
choices sometimes escape us.
We know she'd rather swim in a sunken pond,
gulp minnows from a pocket of mud.
She couldn't know that trapping her
in your cold ceramic tub, rubbing stinging
ointment on her shell, was meant to help.
It's snowing, thick as rotting scutes she shed.
My break ended last week, so I left
again, south toward books and warmth—
I know the injections got harder without help.
That last morning, you chipped every piece of ice
off my windshield as I bid the turtle farewell.
This morning, I wonder if you thought of me
by her box, waiting for absolution.

Letter from the Airport at Midnight

The runway winks in rhythm:
yellow, red. Green, blue.

Flickers speak a code I can't follow
—cues of stop, slow, you're free to go.

Christmas lights through the dark
when I flick off the final lamp

and sit on the other side of the room
for an hour, thinking.

So many nights spent
on different ends of this land.

When I drive away from her, the highway
lifts into stars, spirals through

plastic yellow giants orbiting asphalt.
Solo flights go slowest.

As tarmac lights blur
into a control panel, I can't find

the switch that'll fix my heading.
I only hope we make it home.

Epithalamion

For J.B.

> Now lay those sorrowfull complaints aside,
> And having all your heads with girland crownd,
> Helpe me mine owne loves prayses to resound,
> Ne let the same of any be envied . . .
> —Edmund Spenser

This morning, the leaves were Army gold
as fall first crossed into Atlanta.
At the pavilion in the park, I picked up
a few that'd fallen on the grass,
laid them back on the railing and thought
of an arbor in this same early stillness,
its wood cool and dappled with shadow,
awaiting a procession. You,
behind the silver satins and deep red silks,
light of the gowns glancing off live oaks
that edge a green lawn. Men draped
with earth shades follow behind
the niece all in pink. Your hand
on your father's elbow. You see him, waiting,
but in your eye,
                the arbor
meets a second sky where a summer arch
twirled with fairy lights casts disco shades
across the white of her gown, and yours
when you reach her. Her fingers in the morning,
in every morning together: warmed by a teacup
or you. She slips you a daisy and disappears
behind an eyelid. Step forward:
his haystack hair and tux, this one you've chosen.

You were one of us. I watched you chase
rebounds, hit layups, kiss your girl quick before
sprinting to half court. We danced the sticky floor
at Coconuts with drag kings whose beards
sagged in the heat. After my split, after I left
the fold, I quilted your memories in t-shirt squares
backed in Army gold. We haven't talked
since I left it with you, but I see your photos:
him, and him, and both of you an iceberg
in the sea of our friends' faces.
Their smiles say nothing. But I feel something
turn in my gut as I see them in silence
beside my love: the vision of my wedding skirts yours,
or what I know yours must be, for you
have gone the other way. The love
I embraced, I fear. Is it real, or the long dream
of a false desire? It could vanish as yours did.
Will my mind
                  straighten itself out over years
to some truer nature? I can't watch
you moving up the aisle, can't abide the size
of his hand over yours, can only fling
a handful of rice to the pavilion floor.
All I see are my leaves, resting a moment
before swirling on a breeze that floats them
across the lake. They settle on the dark water,
submerge, and are gone.

Unearthed

What we buried stayed deep beneath tidy-edged beds,
rose faces bright and upturned, looking sunward
from emerald lawns. We scrawled gel pens across
paper scraps, pushed them into root beds.
We scraped through dirt and pine straw, touched lips
to soil before smothering our whispers to stop
their escape. I thought to bury my whole self
and let the earth melt flesh—let me rise, unburdened
of so much weight. Slim, like the older girl
whose ponytail I followed from across the gym.
Words that slid over the pleather bus seats,
pursued me home, and sat in a corner, waiting.
Secret knowledge of our bodies. Games played
in the shadows of trees. Longings we knew as unfit
among neat shuttered duplexes, pushed deep down.
But the Earth never destroys, only remakes.
Even now, a maple's admonition: *I know. You knew.*

Plaza in Late Spring

Kansas City, MO

The warthog's scalding nose pinks my skin,
and the fountains bubble warm in this heatwave
as your hometown's sun sears our arms.

Gold, the dome rising amid hot ochre roofs—
ghosts of prairie grass pinned under the asphalt—
false basilica in the shopping district where

you point out the vine-leafed cornets
below the gutters, the fan-lattice balconies
on storefronts, the blue and yellow tiles tessellating

throughout the streets. You shrug as I point out
the wrought-iron *XXI Forever* and the incidental neon.
By the Nichols fountain, a woman paints

this stretch of skyline without streetlights
or high-rises, just spire and tile and stone:
time and slow brushstrokes

untwine contradictions that fit.
Feet in the water, you talk about Christmastime,
when a different color frames each building,

and snow thickens on the stucco. *We'll be back.
Together,* you promise, and we walk on
as silent belfries gape at the passing cars.

About the Author

Jocelyn Heath is an Associate Professor in English at Norfolk State University. Her poem "Orbital" won the 2014 Allison Joseph Poetry Award from *Crab Orchard Review*. Her creative writing has also appeared in *The Atlantic, Poet Lore, Sinister Wisdom, Flyway, Fourth River,* and elsewhere. Her book reviews have appeared at Lambda Literary, *Grist, Tinderbox, Southeast Review, Entropy,* and *The Lit Pub*. She is an Assistant Editor for *Smartish Pace*.

www.ingramcontent.com/pod-product-compliance
Lightning Source LLC
Chambersburg PA
CBHW071011160426
43193CB00012B/2009